The Elementary School Teacher's
Learning Guide for

The Case
of the
Missing Tutu!

SHARA PUGLISI KATSOS

Learning Guide
created by
KARA LYNCH, BA, MAT

Illustrated by John Bulens

Visit us at
www.facebook.com/Doggie.Investigation.Gang
www.digthebooks.com

Copyright 2019 by Shara Puglisi Katsos
Doggie Investigation Gang, DIG ™
By Shara Puglisi Katsos
Learning Guide by Kara Lynch, BA, MAT
Illustrations by John Bulens
Published by Katman Productions, LLC
Edited by Tanya Gold
ISBN 978-0-578-44971-5

Printed in the United States of America

January 2019

This book is dedicated to all the aspiring dancers and their dance teachers. Believe in yourself and keep following the music in your heart!

Learning Guide

This learning guide is meant to complement a young reader's experience as they navigate their way through the text. The following are a few objectives from the corresponding Grade Three Common Core Standards that this learning guide touches upon.

> RL.1 Students will describe the characters in a story and explain how their actions contribute to the story's events.

> RF.4c Students will use strategies to understand unknown words.

> SL.2 Students will determine the main idea and supporting details of a text.

> L.4 Students will determine or identify the meaning of unknown and multiple meaning words or phrases based on Grade Three reading and content, choosing flexibly from a range of strategies.

> L.4d Students will use glossaries or beginning dictionaries both print and digital to determine or clarify the precise meaning of keywords and phrases.

A section of this guide will follow each chapter of the book. Each chapter includes a pre-reading and post-reading assignment to assist in learning in a creative manner.

Contents

Introduction

There has been a new addition to the Doggie Investigation Gang Family! What do you think it could be? A kitten? Nope! A puppy? Great guess, but nope! A human girl? You are correct! A human girl, named Sophie!

Join the Doggie Investigation Gang in their new Series of Adventures! Get ready, and hold on to your tails as we begin Series Two!

Introduction

Post-Reading

There is some exciting news about a very special addition to the Doggie Investigation Gang family. Sophie is here! Take a moment to close your eyes and visualize (imagine a picture in your mind) this special little girl. What do you think Sophie will do in this book? Be sure to include some details about what she looks like and how she might fit into the gang.

Missing

"The toddler is crying, the toddler is crying!" yelled Charlie.

"We hear her, Charlie. We hear her!" shouted Pedro.

"What could be wrong? Our sweet Sophie is sad."

"Let's find out," replied Cooper.

Cooper, Charlie and Pedro quickly ran through the kitchen, up the stairs, and sat in the doorway to Sophie's bedroom. They heard their mom trying to console three-year-old Sophie.

Sophie's usually sparkling blue eyes were soft and dulled from tears streaming down her cheeks. Their mom was kneeled down beside her as Sophie hugged her tight and spoke of her favorite tutu.

The pups could tell by Sophie's ballet tights and slippers that today was Saturday. Sophie and their mom were getting ready for Sophie's weekly ballet class, but something was missing, her purple tutu.

After assessing the situation, Cooper looked at Charlie and nodded to the stairs. Cooper gently put his front right paw on Pedro's shoulder to suggest that they go down to the kitchen.

Cooper led the way. Charlie and Pedro followed to the kitchen.

"Her purple sparkly tutu with the big purple bow," said Charlie. "It's missing."

"That's her favorite tutu!" exclaimed Pedro with concern in his voice.

"Yes, it is," replied Cooper. "She has so many tutus. I bet she has a tutu in every color of the rainbow. But she treasures this tutu because her friend Katelyn gave it to her."

"Katelyn, isn't she the talented dancer who won all those competitions? No wonder, Sophie treasures that tutu. Poor Sophie, we need to help Mom find it!" said Pedro.

"Where do we even begin to look?" cried Charlie. "Sophie has the energy of a puppy! It could be anywhere."

"You're right, Charlie," Cooper agreed, "but we do have experience with some pretty tough cases. I mean after all, we found Duchess, right? And, you and Pedro befriended turtles to help us when we were looking for Bianca's pendant. We can do this."

"Definitely!" Charlie and Pedro shouted in unison. "We got this!"

"Another mystery, Wahoo!" yelled Pedro as he excitedly did his little happy spin. "Let's think about this and where the tutu could be!"

Cooper, Charlie and Pedro huddled by their water bowl, their favorite spot to brainstorm. They tried to remember the last time they saw Sophie in the purple tutu.

"Was it Monday?" asked Cooper.

"No, no," replied Charlie. "Monday was pasta night. Sophie did not have her tutu on that day. I remember because she got tomato sauce all over her pretty pink dress."

"Tuesday?" asked Cooper.

"Nope, it was Saturday!" Pedro exclaimed proudly. "I remember she was dancing all over the kitchen and she kept twirling by me. The tutu material is unmistakable. It smells like Sophie's baby shampoo. Every time it brushes my nose as she twirls by me, it makes my nose tingle like I'm going to sneeze! She was practicing before her dance class."

"Pedro you're a genius!" yelled Charlie.

The dogs high fived, excited for their next mystery-solving adventure.

Chapter 1: Missing

Pre-Reading

The following vocabulary words will be
used in this chapter. Look up word meanings
in a dictionary and discuss what you find.
Can you make a real-life connection to one
of these words?

console

assessing

situation

Post-Reading, Text Talk

Answer the questions below about the chapter that you just read. You can work with a partner to make it more fun!

1. What details on page 2 does the author use to show the reader that Sophie is extremely upset?

2. Go back to page 3. How did the pups know it was Saturday? Which detail on page 5 shows that the dogs had a positive attitude towards this new challenge? Pedro relies on his sense of smell, as he is unable to see. What smell helps him remember the tutu's material? Write about something that you remember because of its scent.

Hope

"Pedro, you use your fast smelling nose to search the house. I will go in the back yard and search the premises," Cooper instructed.

"Charlie, you keep watch on Mom and Sophie and alert us to any changes. Try to console Sophie with your cuddles. Let's all report back at the water bowl before dinner."

"On it!" Pedro shouted.

"Me too!" shouted Charlie as he happily ran to Sophie's room. He loved to cuddle. He only wished that Sophie was not feeling sad about her purple tutu, but he knew that the Doggie Investigation Gang would resolve this problem and Sophie would be happily twirling in her purple tutu in no time.

After a few hours passed, the three best friends met at their water bowl as planned.

"Any updates?" Charlie asked Cooper.

"Unfortunately, no good news," Cooper reported reluctantly.

"How about you, Pedro?" asked Cooper.

"Well, I did not find the tutu, but I was able to track down a few scents. If my nose is correct, I believe the tutu

went from Sophie's room, down the stairs, through the living room, through the kitchen to the back door, to the garage and into Mom's car. And that is where the smell stopped."

"Great work, Pedro!" said Charlie. "Maybe the tutu is in Mom's car. We must tell Mom right away and get her to open the car door."

The three dogs ran to their mom happily barking and jumping.

Chapter 2: Hope

Pre-Reading

The following vocabulary words will be used in this chapter. Look up word meanings in a dictionary and discuss what you find. Can you make a real-life connection to one of these words?

premises

alert

resolve

reluctantly

Post-Reading, Text Talk

Answer the questions below about the chapter that you just read. You can work with a partner to make it more fun!

1. What details did Pedro uncover using his sense of smell on page 7? Use these details to draw a map showing all of the places that the tutu went.

2. Think about what might happen. Do you think the Doggie Investigation Gang will find the tutu in their mom's car? Where do you think the tutu might be?

On the Trail

"What is all this commotion about?" Their mom asked with a smirk. "Is it supper time already? It is just about time to start preparing dinner isn't it?" She scooped up Sophie in her arms. "Come on, Sophie."

The three dogs ran ahead of their mom through the kitchen towards the garage.

"Hmm, not dinner. What is it, boys?" She opened the side door to the garage.

All three dogs ran over to the back door of her car.

"You want to go for a ride? Now? What's all this about? Boys, you know it's time to get ready for dinner. I need

to feed Sophie, give her a bath, and
then we have story time and bedtime."
Cooper, Charlie and Pedro all
looked at her without giving up. They
were determined to get her to open the
door.
"Okay," she said, "I do not know
what this is all about, but I will open
the car door." She looked to Sophie
and said maybe they are on the search
for snacks left behind in the car.

Quickly, Cooper jumped in and searched the back seat for the purple tutu. Nothing! He was feeling disappointed. He had been hopeful the purple tutu would be by the car seat, but nothing. Pedro jumped in behind Cooper and used his nose to search for any possible clues. The tutu was definitely not in the car.

"That's it!" Cooper thought. He jumped out of the car and barked with joy. He knew he and his friends were on the trail to finding the purple tutu.

"This is great. Thanks to Pedro's nose we know that the tutu was lost outside of the house. And I think I know where that could be" said Cooper, wagging his long yellow furry tail with excitement. "The Forever Friends Dancing School!"

"Of course! Sophie last wore her tutu to her toddler ballet class on Saturday morning. She must have left it there," said Pedro.

"Now, how do we get there? Mom is never going to take us to dance class," said Charlie with dispair in his voice.

Chapter 3: On the Trail

Pre-Reading

The following vocabulary words will be used in this chapter. Look up word meanings in a dictionary and discuss what you find. Can you make a real-life connection to one of these words?

smirk

determined

despair

Post-Reading, Text Talk

Answer the questions below about the chapter that you just read. You can work with a partner to make it more fun!

1. On page 11, Sophie's mom talks about Sophie's bedtime routine. Make a text-to-self connection. What routine do you have in your own family? Write a few sentences about it.

2. Why does Sophie's mom think the pups want her to open the car door?

3. How do you think the gang is going to convince their mom to take them to The Forever Friends Dance School?

Family Watch Week

As their mom and Sophie were getting ready for dance class, the dogs circled around them.

"What is it, boys?" their mom asked. "You look like you want to come too? Well, today happens to be family watch week. Would you like to

come? I will have to ask Jenn, Sophie's teacher, but I think if the three of you are willing to be quiet and sit still, it will be okay."

All three dogs wagged their tails with excitement and triumph.

On the way to dance class, Sophie giggled with amusement that all three dogs were coming with her.

Cooper, Charlie and Pedro sat with their heads held high beside their ballerina sister. They were so proud to be participating in family watch week. They loved Sophie and felt honored to be part of her family.

When they arrived to class, they all walked into the school on their best behavior. The waiting room was bursting with excitement. It was filled with happy dancing toddlers waiting for the moment that they could rush into the dance studio. There were parents, grandparents and siblings all excited for family watch week.

Cooper, Charlie and Pedro were the only dogs. They were quite overjoyed, but did not let that interfere with the work that needed to be done. Charlie and Cooper immediately began scanning the waiting room for any unclaimed purple tutus as Pedro sniffed the floor for any potential clues. They even looked in the lost and found bin, which seemed to have even more shoes than their mom's closet.

"No luck," Pedro said, sighing. "Not even a clue for me to sniff."

The dogs watched the dancers perform their routine for their families, who were beaming with pride. In the corner of the studio, Cooper, Charlie and Pedro looked gloomy.

They stayed for the class and then followed their mom back to the waiting room. While Sophie put on her jacket and said goodbye to her dancing friends, the dogs waited patiently by the school bulletin board.

"Wait a minute," whispered Cooper. "The Forever Friends Dancing School dance troupe is performing in the dance recital with a dancing dog!"

"What?" exclaimed Charlie with a little bit of envy. "Who's the dog?"

"The sign doesn't say, but it's next Saturday night! Let's go and find out!"

"That sounds like a great idea," said Pedro. "It will lift our spirits!"

They followed Sophie and their mom out to the parking lot. As they approached the car, they felt a gust of wind.

When the wind hit Pedro's nose, he jumped for joy. He smelled the tutu in the air. "It's here somewhere! It's here!"

Cooper and Charlie watched Pedro and knew by his expression what it all meant. They immediately began to scan the parking lot. Behind the lot was a small forest with a meadow. As he looked around, Charlie could see a sparkly reflection in the water, could it be?

He barked to their mom as she was helping little Sophie into her car seat. She turned and knew that he was asking to walk over to the meadow.

"Charlie, just for a minute. Go ahead, but no swimming. It's just about time to leave," she said.

He tilted his head softly to let her know that he understood.

He looked all around to be certain there were no cars and then ran to the meadow with Cooper.

When he got there, he knew he was right. There was a sparkly reflection.

Cooper and Charlie looked up to find the source. They could see a purple sash and just a hint of sequined tutu hanging out of a hole in the tree.

Cooper and Charlie barked with excitement.

As they barked, a little head with two perky ears hesitantly peered through the hole. It looked at the dogs and quickly pulled the tutu into the tree.

Within a minute, their mom came over to see what the commotion was all about. By then the tutu was no longer in sight.

"What is all the noise about?" she asked Cooper and Charlie.

They barked at the tree with all their might in hopes that their mom would understand.

Unfortunately, she did not. "It is a beautiful autumn day, isn't it? Come on boys, it's time to go home."

Cooper and Charlie did not know what to do. The two dogs quietly jumped in the car. Pedro followed.

On the return home Cooper and Charlie told Pedro what they had seen as Sophie napped in her car seat beside them.

"This is a dilemma," Pedro said, distress in his voice. "Are you certain it was the tutu? Was it a small monster in the tree that took the tutu?"

"What's the plan now, Cooper?" Charlie asked.

"I don't know," Cooper said. He was concerned that they would not be able to return the tutu to their dear Sophie after all.

"But, you always have a plan, Cooper," Pedro said.

Chapter 4: Family Watch Week

Pre-Reading

The following vocabulary words will be used in this chapter. Look up word meanings in a dictionary and discuss what you find. Can you make a real-life connection to one of these words?

triumph

interfere

scanning

potential

envy

troupe

gust

Post-Reading, Text Talk

Answer the questions below about the chapter that you just read. You can work with a partner to make it more fun!

1. What did Sophie do on page 15 to show how she felt about the dogs coming to dance class?

2. What does Pedro mean when he says "It will lift our spirits?" Explain this expression in your own words.

3. Why does Pedro jump for joy at the end of page 17?

4. Good readers use different information to comprehend a story. This includes looking closely at illustrations. Look at page 19. Can you tell from the illustration why the tutu is no longer in sight? Time is an important part of a story's setting. What does the dogs' mom say to reveal what time of year it is?

5. What kind of plan do you think the Doggie Investigation Gang will come up with to get the tutu back?

A Dear Friend

Upon returning home, the dogs went outside and sat on their deck. Their mom had been right. It was a beautiful, warm, sunny fall day. There was a light breeze and a bright blue sky without a cloud to be seen. The air smelled like October. It was one of the dogs' favorite times of year, yet even this beautiful autumn day was not helping to lift their mood. All they could think about was the small monster in the tree that held Sophie's tutu captive.

"What's with all the long faces?" their dear young friend Chloe the catbird asked sweetly as she flew over and perched herself on their deck.

Cooper told her all about the

missing tutu, the Forever Friends
Dancing School visit, and the small
monster in the tree.

"I've never seen a monster in a tree
before," she said, a little shaken. "I've
seen lots of trees, but I've never seen a
monster in one. What did this monster
look like?"

"Well, it had a small head with two
small ears," Charlie said.

"Wait, did it have brown fur with
two small eyes and a small tail?" asked
the bird.

"I think so," replied Charlie.

"Thank goodness," said Chloe with a sigh of relief. "I don't think that was a monster. It sounds like a chipmunk to me. They are charming little critters."

"It took Sophie's tutu," Cooper said with a hint of anger in his voice. He was always protective of his little Sophie and was not happy that any critter, sweet or not, small or big, would take something that she loved away from her. "It doesn't seem charming to me."

Pedro and Charlie sat quietly. It was not like Cooper to sound angry. They were worried about their friend.

"I understand that you are all upset," said Chloe with empathy in her voice. "But this has to be a misunderstanding. A chipmunk would not hurt a fly. They live in trees and scurry for nuts. I don't know what they would want with a tutu."

"And, now we will never find out. Family Day at the Forever Friends Dancing School will not happen again for a whole year. How would we ever convince mom to take us to a regular dance class? We failed our Sophie," Charlie replied, his voice somber.

All three dogs felt defeated.

"What am I hearing?" Chloe was baffled by her friends' willingness to give up on a case. "This is not like the Doggie Investigation Gang. I will not have it. Sometimes, you just need some help from your friends. And in this case, I think a friend that can fly like me would be just what you need to help you. Sophie is a thoughtful girl who never forgets to fill the bird-feeders. I would be honored to help get her tutu back."

"Thank you, Chloe," said Cooper. "You're right! With friends like you we can solve this problem. I have a plan."

Chapter 5: A Dear Friend

Pre-Reading

The following vocabulary words will be used in this chapter. Look up word meanings in a dictionary and discuss what you find. Can you make a real-life connection to one of these words?

captive

empathy

somber

misunderstanding

baffled

Post-Reading, Text Talk

Answer the questions below about the chapter that you just read. You can work with a partner to make it more fun!

1. Read the first paragraph on page 23. What details help you visualize (imagine a picture in your mind) the day? Draw a small picture of the type of day as you see it.

2. What new character enters the story on page 23?

3. What useful skill does this character have that could help the pups get the tutu back?

4. Go back to page 27 and find the character trait that is used to describe Sophie. What example is given to show this trait?

Take Flight

Following Cooper's plan, the next morning, Chloe flew to the Forever Friends Dancing School and looked all around for the tree with the hole by the meadow.

Her small wings were beginning to tire. It wasn't as easy as she had thought it would be to find the tree. There happened to be a number of trees with holes behind the dancing school building. But she did not want to let her friends down.

She decided to take a break and drink some water from the meadow. As she sat in the autumn sun by the streaming water, she noticed a sparkly reflection in the water. It was an extraordinary shade of purple. Chloe looked up, following the reflection. As her eyes reached the top of the tree, she saw what she had traveled so far for.

Chloe slowly flew up to the hole. She remembered that Cooper and Charlie said that they'd seen a monster. Even though she reminded herself that it was just a chipmunk, her little feathers fluttered in fear. What if she was wrong and they were right?

As quietly as possible, she flew around the hole, peeking in. She tried to use caution in case she needed to make a fast getaway.

She could see the sparkly purple material inside. She looked for any signs of a monster, but all she could see were acorns, leaves and some strange robotic looking appliances. She sighed in relief. It did not look like the home of a monster. In fact, it was quite tidy.

Using her beak, she gently tapped on the bark of the tree. As she did, a head peeked out from the material of

the tutu. This is certainly not a
monster. It was too cute. Chloe
chuckled to herself, and although she
would not admit it to others, she was
very relieved.

Chapter 6: Take Flight

Pre-Reading

The following vocabulary words will be used in this chapter. Look up word meanings in a dictionary and discuss what you find. Can you make a real-life connection to one of these words?

reflection

extraordinary

Post-Reading, Text Talk

Answer the questions below about the chapter that you just read. You can work with a partner to make it more fun!

1. Why wasn't it as easy as Chloe thought to locate the tree?

2. What detail on page 28 tells us that Chloe is getting worn out?

3. What adjective (describing word) does Chloe use on page 30 to describe the creature in the tree?

An Unusual Companion

"Hello," Chloe said to the chipmunk in a gentle voice. She did not want to startle the small animal.

"Good day," replied the chipmunk with the boldness of a big grizzly bear.

Chloe was surprised at the chipmunk's boldness. She instantly found him interesting and engaging. "My name is Chloe," she said with kindness in her voice.

"My name is Sebastian," he said as he dressed himself in a rugged looking brown coat with dark tan patches on the elbows of his sleeves. His pants were a light brown and looked firmly pressed. He held a gold frame monocle to his left eye. Attached to the monocle was a chain that descended into his

coat pocket. Completing the outfit was
a black top hat that looked like it had
been once a toy hat for a doll. His
outfit made him appear quite clever.

"Sebastian, it is very nice to meet you. I've traveled a great distance to find you for my friends, the Doggie Investigation Gang. They noticed that you might have an item that belongs to their sister, Sophie. It is a purple, sparkly tutu. It's her favorite and she lost it at the Forever Friends Dancing School." She pointed with her beak to the building behind them. "She is sad and misses it greatly."

"Oh," replied Sebastian. "I do not know what a tu-to is and I can assure you that I do not have it."

"A tutu,"gently corrected Chloe, "is made of a soft, and delicate fabric. It looks like the item you have over there in your home."

"Oh, you mean my tree slider. I found it on the ground by that school. I'm an inventor. And I am using it to invent a safe, and more efficient way for chipmunks like myself to travel from their home to the ground," he said proudly. "I cannot tell you how many times I have tried to get to an acorn before a squirrel. Squirrels are quite fast, you know. They have longer legs than chipmunks. The tree slider gives me an advantage. I hope to share my invention with chipmunks across the world!" he said as he looked off into the distance, hope and ambition in his voice.

Chloe was speechless. She had never made the acquaintance of a chipmunk quite like this one before. He was an ambitious inventor. She didn't want to hurt his feelings by laughing, but he was just the cutest animal she ever met. But clearly, it was not going to be easy to get Sophie's tutu back.

Chapter 7: An Unusual Companion

Pre-Reading

The following vocabulary words will be
used in this chapter. Look up word meanings
in a dictionary and discuss what you find.
Can you make a real-life connection to one
of these words?

startle

boldness

engaging

monocle

advantage

efficient

acquaintance

ambitious

Post-Reading, Text Talk

Answer the questions below about the chapter that you just read. You can work with a partner to make it more fun!

1. In order to show the character trait of boldness, what animal does the author compare the chipmunk to on page 31?

2. What special job does Sebastian have?

3. Sebastian has a very unique name for the tutu. What does he call it? Describe what helps him do.

4. Based on her interactions with Sebastian, does Chloe think it will be easy or difficult to get the tutu back? What text detail tells you this?

A Dark Night

Chloe asked Sebastian if she might enter his home. She explained that her wings were getting tired from fluttering outside and that she had an interesting story to tell him.

"I do love an interesting story. Please come in. Where are my manners, would you like some acorn tea?"

"That would be lovely," replied Chloe.

Chloe lowered her head to enter the hole in the tree. She sat down by Sebastian's table made of a thick tree branch. She was in awe of all the items in his home. There were what looked to be inventions everywhere.

As she begin to tell Sebastian all

about the Doggie Investigation Gang
and all of their adventures, she
realized that Sebastian was not making
the sweet tea and biscuits she could
smell. Instead, there were small
inventions making the snacks for them.

"That's amazing!" Chloe
exclaimed, completely losing track of
her story. "Your inventions are making
our tea and biscuits!"

There was a robot-like invention

placing small leaves in cups of warm
water and an arm looking invention
placing small balls of dough on a
warm leaf above a small fire. She was
very impressed.

Sebastian was so happy to share
his inventions with her. He told her all
about his early inventions, ones that
had failed and his successes. He was
as proud of his failures as he was of
the inventions that were used by all the

chipmunks in the area. Chloe was having such a great time she didn't realize that dusk was drawing near.

"I am so sorry," Chloe said. "I must be going. I truly enjoyed my visit with you. I am so grateful to have met you."

"The feeling is mutual, my dear new friend, Chloe," Sebastian replied. "Please take the tu-to, is that what you called it? Anyway, please take it with you and do come back again to visit."

"A tutu," replied Chloe.

"Yes, such a strange name," he replied. "Anyway, please bring it back to your friends. They sound like a kind group of dogs and I would hate to be the cause of their sadness. I will certainly find another way to invent a tree slider for chipmunks."

"Thank you so much for the tutu and your generosity. The tea and biscuits were magnificent," replied Chloe. She hugged her new friend with her wings and gently placed the ribbon of the tutu in her mouth. She was a little worried. It was heavier than she thought it would be.

As Chloe flew back to the Doggie Investigation Gang, the autumn moon was rising. She did not often fly at night, but she was eager to get home and share her news with Cooper, Charlie and Pedro. She knew they would be happy to see her and the tutu.

Chapter 8: Dark Night

Pre-Reading

The following vocabulary words will be used in this chapter. Look up word meanings in a dictionary and discuss what you find. Can you make a real-life connection to one of these words?

awe

dusk

generosity

magnificent

Post-Reading, Text Talk

Answer the questions below about the chapter that you just read. You can work with a partner to make it more fun!

1. What did Chloe see when she entered Sebastian's home?

2. What was Chloe amazed by after Sebastian offered her a snack?

3. What unique inventions in Sebastian's home are described on pages 36 and 37? Draw what you think they would look like.

4. On page 37, we learn that Sebastian is as proud of his failures as he is of his successes. Make a text-to-self connection. When did you fail only to later go on to achieve success? Write a few sentences about that time.Use your own words to describe Sebastian's actions on page 38 when it was time for Chloe to leave. What character traits can we infer (know without directly being told) from these actions?

The Search Continues

By the time Chloe arrived, the dogs had already gone to bed and her mood had changed. Somewhere along the flight back to the house, she had dropped the tutu. She had miscalculated the weight and had not planned on the darkness.

The next morning, when the Doggie Investigation Gang went outside, she told them about her trip.

She told them about the chipmunk, Sebastian, his inventions, the snacks his inventions made, and his plans for the tutu. And she told them about the flight home and how she dropped the tutu in the dark.

"Do you mean it wasn't a monster?" asked Pedro.

"Not at all, Pedro," replied Chloe.

"That's fantastic," Pedro said with a sigh of relief.

"We are just so glad that you are home safe, Chloe," said Cooper. "Don't worry. We will find the tutu. Thank you for being such a loyal friend."

Chloe assured the pups that she and her bird friends would fly the route she had taken home to look for the tutu.

"We will search as well," said Charlie. "We will put our noses to the ground!"

As day turned into night, the dogs and the birds could not find any clues as to where the tutu might be. After midnight the Doggie Investigation Gang and their friends decided to end the search and retreat to bed. Chloe and her winged friends promised Cooper, Charlie and Pedro that they would continue their search during daylight hours.

Chapter 9: The Search Continues

Pre-Reading

The following vocabulary words will be used in this chapter. Look up word meanings in a dictionary and discuss what you find. Can you make a real-life connection to one of these words?

miscalculated

loyal

assured

retreated

Post-Reading, Text Talk

Answer the questions below about the chapter that you just read. You can work with a partner to make it more fun!

1. Why did Chloe's mood change at the beginning of Chapter 9? What adjective does Cooper use to describe what kind of friend Chloe is?

2. What do Chloe and the dogs promise at the end of Chapter 9?

Dance Recital

As days turned into a week, the tutu was still not found. It was now Saturday night, the night of the dance recital. Sophie was excited to perform on stage with her friends from her dance class for the first time. She was also excited to see her older friend Katelyn and her cousin Lexi making their debut in the Forever Friends Dancing School senior dance troupe.

Cooper and Charlie were eager to see Sophie dance, and even more so to see the performance of the dancing dog. Pedro was nestled in his seat. Sitting on either side of him were Charlie and Papa Joe. Pedro was ready for Charlie's step by step updates of the dancer's moves and for Papa Joe's snacks.

Although the dogs were discouraged since they had not found the tutu yet, they were excited to see who the mystery dancing dog could be.

As the curtain drew and the music started, the dogs' hearts began to race with excitement. They loved a dance performance.

As the first dance began, Charlie exclaimed in surprise, "Sookie!"

"Shhh, Charlie. We're at a show, but what about Grammy and Grandpa's dog?" Pedro whispered back.

"She's on stage. I didn't know she could dance! She's really twirling on her toes!" Cooper whispered back, trying to control his excitement.

"It's a pirouette. And, the dancers finished their routine in an arabesque, plié and curtsy," whispered Charlie in Pedro's ear without hesitation.

"How do you know all that, Charlie?" asked Pedro.

"Ms Jenn taught me a few steps during my puppy days."

The three dogs stayed late in the concert hall to cheer for Sophie and their friend Sookie.

The show was wonderfully entertaining! There was a variety of tap, ballet and jazz dances. Sophie and her classmates were adorable in a toddler dance.

For the final number, the dance troupe performed a Broadway number. And at the very end of the dance, their friend Sookie had a solo.

As she began her solo, Cooper's and Charlie's jaws dropped simultaneously.

"Do you see what I see?" Charlie asked Cooper.

"I do! It's the purple tutu with the

sparkles! Sookie is wearing Sophie's tutu!"

"The tutu is found! How did it end up in the show?" asked Pedro.

"I have no idea," replied Cooper. "But we will find out."

After the show, the dogs brought Sophie and her friends, Cambelle, Lexi, Katelyn and Sookie, each a bouquet of flowers to congratulate them on their performance. And they gave all the Forever Friends Dancing School directors, Ms Jenn, Ms Kerry and Ms Jess, hugs for letting them attend the show.

As Cooper gave Sookie the colorful flowers, he gently took Sookie's front paw and steered her away from the crowd. Charlie and Pedro followed behind.

As they arrived to a quiet corner of the auditorium lobby, Cooper kindly asked Sookie where she got her tutu.

"Isn't it beautiful?" she said. "I woke up one morning, went outside and there it was in the middle of my yard. Weird, right? I love it though!"

Pedro giggled with happiness. He couldn't believe the luck! Chloe had flown over Grammy and Grandpa's house on her way home from Sebastian's tree, and it must have landed in their yard.

Cooper, Charlie and Pedro told Sookie the entire story.

"Wow, I want to meet this Sebastian someday," Sookie said with amazement and a hint of sadness. Of course, she wanted to return the tutu to its rightful owner, Sophie, but she did really love it. She felt like a unique purple, sparkly star when she performed in it. Sookie, being the sweet dog that she was, gave the tutu to Cooper.

Sensing Sookie's mixed emotions,

Cooper, Charlie and Pedro gave Sookie a comforting hug and thanked her for being such a dear friend.

Upon arriving home, Sophie and her parents began setting the table and preparing dinner. While Sophie was placing the plates on the table, Cooper walked over to her with the purple tutu in his mouth. With Charlie and Pedro by his side, Cooper placed the tutu at Sophie's feet. Sophie squealed with delight so loudly that her parents ran over to see what had happened.

Sophie was so excited to have her tutu back, but even more so that it came from her favorite pups. She immediately hugged all three dogs and gave them each a kiss on the head. Their mom and dad watched with amazement.

"How did they ever find that tutu?" said their dad to their mom.

Before, their mom could reply, Sophie yelled, "they're the Doggie Investigation Gang!"

Their parents giggled. Sophie

danced and twirled in her found tutu.
Cooper, Charlie and Pedro sat happily
wagging their tails and watching their
Sophie dance.

Later that evening, during story time, Sophie, still wearing her tutu, was sitting listening to her mom read when she noticed that there was dog fur on the tutu that looked like Sookie's.

"Mom," said Sophie. "I wonder if Sookie used this for her show last night." She brought the tutu closer to her mom to show her.

"Maybe," their mom said. "I know Sookie loves tutus like you. Maybe it would be fun if we made Sookie a tutu for her next show. Grammy knows how to make tutus and I am certain she would not mind teaching us how."

The next time Grammy came to visit, she taught Sophie how to make a tutu. Together, they made Sookie a purple, sparkly tutu just like hers.

As Cooper, Charlie and Pedro watched the tutus being made, Charlie had an idea.

Charlie took a piece of leftover ribbon from the floor and,with Cooper and Pedro following, brought

it to Chloe outside. Cooper, Pedro and
Chloe were overjoyed with Charlie's
idea.

The next morning, as Charlie
requested, Chloe brought the ribbon to
Sebastian for his tree slider inventions.
Sebastian was grateful and asked her
to thank her dog friends for him.

Mom and Sophie wrapped up the
tutu in pink tissue paper and placed it
in a pink gift bag for Sookie. Sophie
added a little note to the bag, which
read, "For Sookie, I can't wait to see
your next performance with your new
tutu!"

Chapter 10: Dance Recital

Pre-Reading

The following vocabulary words will be used in this chapter. Look up word meanings in a dictionary and discuss what you find. Can you make a real-life connection to one of these words?

perform

routine

hesitating

sensing

emotions

Post-Reading, Text Talk

Answer the questions below about the chapter that you just read. You can work with a partner to make it more fun!

1. Is the process of locating the tutu short or long? What detail at the top of page 43 helps you figure this out?

2. What causes Cooper's and Charlie's jaws to drop on pages 46 and 47?

3. How did the dogs congratulate Sophie and her friends and thank the dance directors? What character traits can you infer (know without being directly told) about the Doggie Investigation Gang based on this action?

4. How does Sophie show her excitement on page 50 when Cooper places the tutu at her feet?

5. What does Sophie notice later, during story time?

6. What is the act of kindness that Sophie and her grammy perform at the end of the page 52?

Encore

The next time the Doggie Investigation Gang, Sophie and their parents visited Grammy and Grandpa, they brought Sookie a surprise. On their way over, they made a quick stop at their favorite local ice cream shop drive-thru, Lickadee Licks, and purchased a gallon of ice cream.

When they arrived at Grammy and Grandpa's house, they could see Sookie in the window. She jumped with excitement when she saw the car and all her friends. Grammy and Grandpa opened the door, smiling, as the entire gang entered the house.

"What's in the pretty bag?" Grandpa asked Sophie.

"This is for Sookie," Sophie replied happily.

Sookie jumped, danced and twirled with happiness when she heard the pretty bag was for her.

Sophie placed the bag on the floor for Sookie to open. Sookie wasted no time and put her nose in the bag. She could not identify the contents by smell, so she ferociously pulled the tissue out of the bag. She stopped with amazement when she saw the purple sparkles. She then gently pulled the tutu from the bag and began to cry with joy. She had her very own sparkly purple tutu, just like her dear friend Sophie's. She was thrilled.

Sookie jumped in Sophie's arms
and gave her the biggest hug a dog
could give. Sophie smiled and giggled.
Everyone laughed as they witnessed
the two girls' happiness.

They all enjoyed their favorite
vanilla Lickadee Licks ice cream. And,
of course, Sophie and Sookie put on
their matching tutus and tap shoes and
performed for their family. Cooper,
Charlie and Pedro were beaming.

THE END

Chapter 11: Encore

Pre-Reading

The following vocabulary words will be used in this chapter. Look up word meanings in a dictionary and discuss what you find. Can you make a real-life connection to one of these words?

identify

ferociously

witnessed

Post-Reading, Text Talk

Answer the questions below about the chapter that you just read. You can work with a partner to make it more fun!

1. How did Sookie thank Sophie for the very kind gift?

2. In the story, happiness follows kindness. This is often true in life as well. Draw a picture of the final story scene in the space below. Be sure to include details from the text. Don't forget the yummy vanilla ice cream!

Reader's Reflection

Which character do you identify most with?
Take a moment and jot down some notes
about each one.

Cooper:

Charlie:

Pedro:

Chloe:

Sookie:

Sebastian:

Sophie:

The Sparkling
Glimmer of Kindness

Think about the many examples of kindness woven throughout the text. It's everywhere! It can be seen in the way the dogs work diligently to console their sweet Sophie when they first hear that her tutu is lost. Kindness also sparkles in the way Chloe speaks to Sebastian about getting the tutu back and the way the dogs handle the news that, after finding the tutu, Chloe dropped it, losing it again. Of course kindness glimmers in the way that the gang approaches Sookie about getting the tutu back. Finally, it's Sophie's kindness that sparkles in making Sookie her very own tutu.

Make a text-to-self connection. Think about a time when you were kind to someone else. Write about this time using details to explain what made this act of kindness so memorable.

About the
Doggie Investigation Gang

Cooper is a yellow labrador retriever. He has a knack for adventure and enjoys swimming and playing catch with his family. Cooper is a certified therapy dog who has been known to visit Veterans at nearby Veterans Administration Hospitals. He enjoys meeting America's heroes and thanking them for their service.

Charlie is a cocker spaniel. His hobbies include walking and swimming. He enjoys hanging out and watching movies with his family. Charlie is also a certified therapy dog who enjoys new people to love and cuddle.

CHARLIE

Pedro is a minpin. He was rescued
by PAWS New England from a puppy
mill. As a result of his experience in a
puppy mill he has glaucoma, which
has resulted in his blindness. Pedro
does not let his blindness hinder him
from enjoying his new life with his
adoptive family, which includes his
two brothers, Cooper and Charlie.

Sookie is a 10-year old female
Maltese. She was adopted from
rescue in February of 2018. Sookie
loves to go for her daily walks and
enjoys her nap times. She enjoys being
with her human pack and cuddling
with them as much as possible.

About the Authors

Shara Katsos was awarded the third highest honor with the Department of the Army Civilian Awards, the Outstanding Civilian Service Award, for substantial contributions to the U.S. Army and Veteran community.

She has a Master of Social Work degree and is a licensed independent social worker. She is employed at the Veterans Healthcare Administration (VHA).

In her children's book series she hopes to inspire children to believe in themselves and to help others. She believes that dogs are a tremendous resource for humans, which dogs have proven through their work leading the blind, assisting the deaf, building confidence for children with autism and Veterans with PTSD. She believes humans should return the favor and make high kill shelters illegal.

She has written the Doggie

Investigation Gang, DIG series in an effort to raise funds for dog rescue groups.

Her hobbies include spending time with her husband, Steve, their daughter, Sophie, and the Doggie Investigation Gang.

Kara Lynch has a Bachelor of Art in Education and a Master of Art in Teaching. She is a Fifth Grade English Language Arts teacher and has been teaching in The Worcester Public School System for 19 years. She has received awards and recognition for her work with students on the Autism Spectrum. Her favorite thing in the world is being a mom to Jack, Joseph, Juliette, and her four-legged baby, a Cavalier King Charles Spaniel, Mabel Rae. She feels that all children and dogs should be read to, loved and appreciated for the uniqueness. Just like in "The Case of the Missing Tutu!" she believes that sometimes, in our search for what is lost, we discover life's greatest examples of kindness, goodness and love.

About the Illustrator

John Bulens has a Bachelor of Art in Philosophy and an Undergraduate Certificate in Graphic Design. He has been freelancing in graphic design and desktop layout for a number of years. In addition, he enjoys volunteering for an international television show that highlights local artists and comedians. This is the fourth children's book John has illustrated. He is a close friend of the members of the Doggie Investigation Gang.

A Note to the Grown Up(s)

Thank you for your purchase of the Case of the Missing Tutu, the first book in the second series of the Doggie Investigation Gang, DIG Books. The author and illustrator are excited to share that the revenue from sales of this book will be donated to non-profit dog rescue groups.

We are proud to share that since our first publication in 2014, we have been able to make substantial donations to PAWS New England. This was possible through the purchases made by of our customers. We are truly grateful for your support. We hope the young readers are inspired by the dogs of the Doggie Investigation Gang, who teach the importance of teamwork, perseverance and supporting the community.

We very much appreciate your support in our mission and hope to be able to continue supporting dog rescue groups!

To learn more about the Doggie Investigation Gang and the mission of the books and how we provide book readings at schools and events throughout New England, please visit us at www.digthebooks.com

Did you enjoy this story? Keep a look out for the Doggie Investigation Gang's next adventure:

The Case of the Missing Sensei!

Check us out on Facebook at

www.Facebook.com/Doggie.Investigation.Gang